Original title:
Tropical Delights and Dreams

Copyright © 2025 Creative Arts Management OÜ
All rights reserved.

Author: Simon Fairchild
ISBN HARDBACK: 978-1-80581-683-6
ISBN PAPERBACK: 978-1-80581-210-4
ISBN EBOOK: 978-1-80581-683-6

Light Dancing on Still Waters

The sun skips on the pond's bright face,
While frogs in tuxedos start their chase.
A dragonfly holds a tiny feast,
Sharing laughs with a lazy beast.

Ripples giggle, making waves of fun,
As fish in bow ties jump and run.
A splash brings all the friends around,
In this watery ball, joy knows no bound.

The Charm of Fishermen's Tales

With nets all tangled, they begin to boast,
About the fish that got away the most.
His buddy nods and winks an eye,
While seagulls swoop and make them cry.

The lure was huge, or so they claim,
It sparkled bright and danced like a flame.
Yet, in the end, it's the stories we keep,
That hook us tight while the ocean sleeps.

Secrets Cradled by the Atlantic

Upon the shore, the waves conspire,
Whispering secrets of fish and fire.
Shells are gossiping in the sand,
Winking at all – isn't life just grand?

A crab in a snapback struts with pride,
While clams hide their pearls, but never slide.
Laughter echoes from morning till dusk,
In these tides, we find our trust.

Beneath a Canopy of Stars

Stars twinkle like ice cream sprinkles bright,
While frogs start their choir with sheer delight.
The moon's a giant pizza in the sky,
Where dreams are tossed like toppings awry.

Fireflies dance in a wiggly line,
Joining the party, oh-so-divine.
Under this ceiling, we all unite,
In the land of giggles, under starlit night.

Hibiscus Blooms and Moonlit Nights

Under a sky so bright and bold,
Hibiscus giggles, tales unfold.
The moon wears shades, a stylish queen,
While crickets chirp their nightly scene.

Laughter spills from oceans blue,
As stars join in, a glittering crew.
A lantern glows on sandy shores,
While impish waves play silly chores.

Dances of the Coconut Trees

Coconuts sway, a wobbly waltz,
Their antics make the sand grains pulse.
With a twist and turn, they steal the show,
As squirrels join in, putting on a glow.

Palm fronds flutter, a fan so grand,
Whispers of jokes in a breezy band.
The monkeys laugh, in a cheeky spree,
Swinging high, as wild as can be.

A Symphony of Coral and Sand

Coral symphonies beneath the tide,
A fish parade, no place to hide.
Anemones sway, in a splashy dance,
While bottom-feeders steal their chance.

Sand crabs scuttle with a clumsy cheer,
In a race with waves, but can't steer clear.
Seashells chuckle, in hues so bright,
As tides relay tales of playful delight.

Sweet Fragrance of Rainforest Blooms

In the thicket, blooms giggle loud,
While critters form a silly crowd.
The raindrops dance on leafy floors,
As flowers paint their fragrant scores.

Butterflies flutter in a clumsy flight,
Wearing spots like a colorful kite.
Vines tangle up in a knotty mess,
Nature's pranks, we all confess.

Fragments of Paradise Unveiled

In a hammock swung by vines so tight,
My drink's umbrella took off in flight.
A parrot squawked, 'What's for lunch?'
I replied, 'Just seaweed and a punch!'

Coconuts rolling down the beach,
Chasing my hat, oh, what a reach!
A crab walked by with a sassy strut,
I chuckled, 'Crabby, not a chance to glut!'

Sunshine turns my ice cream fast,
I licked it once, then it's gone at last.
The sand sticks to my sunscreened chest,
A sticky hug, I must confess!

Life's a dance with waves and froth,
I trip and fall, but hey, who's got cloth?
With laughter bubbling like ocean foam,
I twirl and spin, this beach feels like home.

Treasure Beneath the Crystal Waves

Snorkeling goggles on my head,
I dove for pearls but found seaweed instead.
A fish waved hello with a friendly grin,
I think he thinks I'm a cousin of fin!

Shells whisper secrets of sandy dreams,
While crabs conspire with sun-kissed beams.
I found a treasure chest, just plain old wood,
Inside was a sandwich, and it smelled quite good!

Jellyfish doing the cha-cha glide,
I boogie while avoiding their prickly pride.
The sand tickles as I take a dip,
With mermaids laughing, I add to the trip!

Sunset paints the sky in pink dance shoes,
While coconut drinks bring forth the blues.
I raise my glass to the friendly breeze,
Oh, the joy of life, just like a tease!

Notes of Coconut and Lime

In a world where pineapples dance,
Coconuts giggle, oh what a chance!
Lime slices jump on a jolly plate,
Laughing lemons, they just can't wait.

Chairs made of palm, swaying to the beat,
Sipping on smoothies, oh what a treat!
Coconuts whisper secrets so sweet,
While mangoes shimmy with sticky feet.

Heights of Paradise

Up in the sky where the seagulls sing,
A parrot tells jokes about everything.
Oranges giggle as they roll down hills,
Bananas in pajamas practicing drills.

The sun wears shades like a funky dude,
Palm trees sway, oh they're in the mood!
A hammock swings, weaving tales at night,
While coconuts juggle, what a sight!

Chasing Rainbows After the Rain

After each sprinkle, colors collide,
Fruits in a race, let's take a ride!
Berries and cherries, they slip and slide,
Giggling together, hearts open wide.

A pineapple frowns, it's lost its hat,
The mango offers a cozy mat.
Laughter erupts, oh what a fuss,
While rainbows mock in the gentle gust.

The Essence of Sea Salt and Sage

Waves crash and tumble, like cows on the move,
Salty air tickles, oh how we groove!
Sage plants gossip in breezy delight,
While fish tell tales under moonlit night.

Seashells are snickering, waves take a break,
The starfish prances, just to partake.
With each silly splash, the world feels so right,
In this world of whimsy, laughter takes flight.

Evening Glow of the Horizon

The sun dips low, a flaming ball,
Banana peels roll down the hall.
A parrot squawks, a cheeky grin,
As waves crash down, let the fun begin.

Tomatoes dance, a salsa beat,
Coconuts roll, not missing a beat.
The beach chairs sway, in salty breeze,
While crabs tap dance with utmost ease.

A hammock sways, a lizard sings,
Flip-flops fly with outstretched wings.
A beach ball bounces, joy takes flight,
Under the glow of the starry night.

Laughter echoes, we shout hooray,
For every silly game we play.
Even in sunset's gentle hold,
The stories we share will never grow old.

Serenity in the Tropics

Palm trees whisper, secrets untold,
As sun-kissed cheeks begin to fold.
A hammock strung between two trees,
Invites us to nap in the balmy breeze.

A monkey swings with sliced bread,
While visions of pancakes dance in our head.
The scent of flowers fills the air,
And bees wear tiny hats with flair.

A smoothie spills with a splat and a splash,
We laugh and giggle, oh what a crash!
Watermelons waddle, lemons slice,
In this paradise, we're feeling nice.

The sunset blushes, a clownfish grins,
As everybody dances, while the music spins.
With every chuckle, joy's parade,
In this tranquil hold, life's sweetest trade.

Nature's Velvet Embrace

Sunlight flickers, a playful tease,
As lizards bask with utmost ease.
A bright-eyed frog leaps with a cheer,
Announcing the start of a vibrant year.

Cocoa beans spill like chocolate dreams,
While sugarcane sways in sweet moonbeams.
Laughter erupts, a chorus so loud,
As we gather close, a merry crowd.

The breezes tug at our silly hats,
Teasing the seagulls, missing their chats.
Pineapples wear little party hats,
While snails join in for laughs and spats.

A sunset serenade, wild and bright,
Frogs croon love songs to the night.
With nature's laughter, pure delight,
We dance together, hearts taking flight.

Stories in the Shadows of Bananas

Under leaves, where shadows play,
A squirrel tells jokes, in its own way.
Bananas giggle, in clusters tight,
Sharing laughter, a fruity delight.

With old vines twisting in good cheer,
The memories bloom, year after year.
A pineapple tells tales of sweet delight,
While mangoes sway, feeling just right.

A breeze whispers secrets known so well,
As turtles join, their stories to tell.
Caught in a riddle, a coconut sighs,
Dreaming of clouds, and pie in the skies.

With each burst of laughter, a party begins,
In the heart of shadows, where joy always wins.
The fruits unite, in mirth they believe,
Together, they dance, and never leave.

Beneath the Starry Canopy

Underneath the twinkling lights,
We found a dance with funky sights.
A coconut fell, rolled to my feet,
I slipped and swirled—what a silly feat!

The moon wore shades, a stylish tease,
While crabs performed their sideways squeeze.
A parrot squawked a joke so loud,
We laughed until we drew a crowd.

The Lure of the Ocean's Embrace

Waves with giggles, laughter swirls,
Splashing sun-kissed boys and girls.
A jellyfish wore a charming hat,
I waved hello, it did just that!

Seashells whispered tales of fun,
Of sandy castles half undone.
A crab in shades, danced to a beat,
It wiggled its bum, oh what a treat!

Secrets of the Sunlit Lagoon

In a lagoon where laughter floats,
Frogs had swimming lessons on little boats.
A fish with flair wore a bowtie bright,
Said, 'Join my swim, it'll be a sight!'

Chasing tadpoles, skipping stones,
We teased the turtles with their groans.
A dragonfly spun in a dance,
And off we went, not taking a chance!

Paradise Found in a Mango Heart

Mangoes piled as sweet as dreams,
They dripped with laughter, sticky creams.
I took a bite, oh what a mess!
With juice on my nose, I must confess!

The dance of fruit flies, quite the show,
They zigzagged by, moving to and fro.
Each bite ignited a juicy cheer,
In sugar-spun bliss, we had no fear!

Island Melodies in the Wind

A parrot sings a silly tune,
While crabs dance under the moon.
The coconuts fall, bumping my head,
I chuckle and wish they were bread.

The hammock sways with a creaky sound,
As iguanas lounge, all around.
Tropical drinks spill like a flood,
My hat's now a soggy old bud.

Palm trees flirt with the vibrant skies,
While surfboards chat, oh what a surprise!
A fish with sunglasses swims by with glee,
I swear it winked right back at me.

All in all, life's a silly race,
Where laughter outshines the sun's bright face.
With each gust, comes another jest,
On this island, I'm truly blessed.

The Taste of Salted Breezes

A seagull snatches my potato chip,
I laugh as it takes its victory trip.
Sandcastles fall, not built to last,
The tide's a rascal, it moves so fast.

I sip my drink with a tiny umbrella,
The waiter's dance? Now, that's a fella!
A turtle glides, looking quite chic,
While I attempt a backflip, oh what a freak!

Beach volleyball turns into a game,
Of who can dive with the goofiest aim.
"Watch out!" I yell as I take a tumble,
The crowd erupts in a fit of grumble.

What flavor's that? Salt and laughter,
Moments of joy, happily ever after.
With sun-kissed skin and a grin so wide,
I'm the clown of the ocean, I'll take it in stride.

Radiant Shores of Serenity

The waves whisper secrets too bright to keep,
As umbrellas tangle in a colorful heap.
Kids giggle as they chase foamy tails,
Building dreams with their sandbox flails.

Sandy toes and a hat that's askew,
I wave to a dolphin, it waved back too!
With a splash and a laugh, the fun never fades,
Even if my sunscreen's long lost in spades.

Footprints lead to a snack stand nearby,
Where the ice cream cone's bigger than my eye.
Melting quickly as I run in delight,
A sticky mess makes it a funny sight.

By the shore, with salty air so rare,
I embrace the moments, free from despair.
With giggles and joy, the sun bows down,
On this radiant shore, I wear the crown.

Enchanted by the Coral Light

Coral castles greet the day's sunrise,
While fish throw parties in their disguise.
A clownfish winks, a mermaid just sighs,
In this underwater world, there are no lies.

Dancing to beats of the rushing tide,
I slip on a mask, let curiosity be my guide.
With bubbles floating, I take a dive,
Where goofy sea turtles laugh and thrive.

A starfish plays chess, no moves to find,
While jellyfish twirl, all intertwined.
Their graceful dance makes the whole reef cheer,
In this silly realm, there's nothing to fear.

As sunset paints colors, vivid and bright,
Underwater wonders continue the night.
With laughter and wonders, we swim with delight,
In this enchanted world, everything feels right.

Serene Sands and Silken Skies

On the shore, I lost my shoe,
The crab claimed it, who knew?
Sunburnt nose, I wave and grin,
Caught a fish, it's a rubber din.

Seagulls squawk, they steal my fries,
Under palm trees, I disguise,
In a hammock, I sway and swing,
Dreaming of the snacks I'll bring.

Beach ball bounces, kids all shout,
A funny dance, I spin about,
Sipping juice, a splash takes flight,
The sandman naps; he's out of sight.

My troubles wash away, I swear,
Until a wave pulls at my hair,
I laugh aloud, this beachy bliss,
Is quite the funny, sunny kiss.

Driftwood Dreams and Starry Nights

Driftwood logs, they want to chat,
Whisper secrets, 'til I sat,
The stars above, they wink and tease,
While I giggle at the breeze.

Astro-aliens on their ship,
Offer me a salty dip,
I dance beneath the twinkling glow,
Trip over sand, oh no, oh no!

Beach bonfires, marshmallows roast,
The ghost of snacks I love the most,
S'mores that laugh and poke their charms,
Melted chocolate in my arms.

A comet zooms, I shout and cheer,
While birds fly by with a sneaky leer,
The ocean sways with giggly glee,
In driftwood dreams, I'm fancy-free.

The Language of Lapping Tides

The waves whisper in bubbly tones,
As clams giggle in their shells, they moan,
The tide talks back, it gives a cheer,
Sandcastles grow, but oh dear, oh dear!

Fish in flip-flops dance around,
Jellybeans bounce on the ground,
A crab moonwalks, slick and slow,
Pretending he's in a rock and roll show.

Shells tell tales of ocean fun,
While I try to catch the sun,
The tides tickle my toes with glee,
I giggle back, "Come play with me!"

Sandy socks and splashes near,
The ocean's laughter fills the air,
In salty waves, we find the rhyme,
Of lapping tides, the best of time.

Paradise Found in Every Coconut

Crack a coconut, joy spills out,
A squirrel cheers, "What's this about?"
I take a sip, it's a silly thrill,
While friends joke, "Just don't get your fill!"

A parrot squawked, "You drink like me!"
Feathers fluffed, he's here with glee,
Jokes and laughs with every bite,
Coconuts roll, oh, what a sight!

Lizards tango in the sun's warm beams,
Chasing dreams that burst at the seams,
I toss a shell, it lands on a shoe,
A style choice? I don't have a clue!

So here's to fun, in every sip,
A coconut's hug with every trip,
In paradise, I dance and sway,
With each coconut, it's a funny day.

Rhythms of the Roaming Waves

The ocean hums a breezy tune,
As crabs dance under the bright full moon.
Seagulls try to steal a round of fries,
While fish wave back with bubble sighs.

Shells all painted like a fancy hat,
A dolphin jokes, 'I'm not your mat!'
Surfboards zooming, folks take flight,
Splashing water, oh what a sight!

The beach ball leaps into the air,
A moment later, it's just not there.
Sandcastles crumble with a laugh,
While kids draw maps for treasure's path.

In this place where giggles leap,
Even sand can make you weep.
Catch a wave or simply stroll,
Life's a jest, let joy take toll!

Secrets of the Sun-Drenched Garden

In the garden blooms a quirky rose,
Wearing polka dots, who knows how it grows?
Bees gather round for a silly dance,
While a snail claims to be 'fast by chance.'

Tomatoes argue, 'I'm the juiciest!'
While cucumbers roll, 'We're the gooiest!'
A bird chirps jokes from up in the tree,
Leaves giggle softly, 'Come join the spree!'

Sunflowers sway, playing hide and seek,
The carrots yell, "Not fair! Take a peek!"
Butterflies flutter in vibrant delight,
While garden gnomes tease, 'Join us, take flight!'

With every bloom, the laughter grows,
In this patch where silliness flows.
Plant a smile, watch it sprout,
Life's just fun, without a doubt!

A Symphony of Exotic Colors

Colors clash like a massive parade,
Grapefruits giggle, 'Look at our shade!'
Mangoes tango, with a wink and a sway,
While bananas slip on a bright sunny day.

Papayas and pineapples join in the fun,
Throwing a party under the blazing sun.
A rainbow tree chuckles, 'I'm the best show!'
While berries drop beats, giving joy as they flow.

The painter's brush gets wild with glee,
As colors swirl like a frothy sea.
Paint splatters, creating vibrant tunes,
A masterpiece of laughter beneath the moons.

With every stroke, they sing a song,
In this world where colors belong.
Join the melody, dance with the spree,
Life's a canvas, just let it be!

Celestial Sunsets and Caramel Skies

At twilight's kiss, the skies blush bright,
Clouds wear cotton candy, oh what a sight!
Birds serenade with a last happy cheer,
Echoing whispers, 'The night's almost here!'

Stars play peek-a-boo, little shiny spies,
As fireflies gossip with twinkling eyes.
The moon tells tales with a knowing grin,
While shadows waltz, the fun begins!

Sandy toes mix with a soft soft breeze,
Chasing twilight while munching on cheese.
With wishes made on every bright star,
Laughter connects us, no matter how far.

Colors swirl as the day fades slow,
In this silly dance, it's the best kind of show.
So lift a toast to the sunset's we see,
Life's a party, just dance wild and free!

Footprints on Sunlit Sands

Footprints giggle as they play,
Dancing on the shore each day.
A crab joins in, a silly scene,
Pinching toes, like a clingy bean.

Children run, they slip and slide,
Chasing waves, with joy as their guide.
Sandy hands, a sculptor's crew,
Creating castles that look like stew.

Seagulls squawk, a humorous chat,
One swoops down, and steals a hat.
Laughter echoes with every splash,
Each moment bright, a silly bash.

Sunsets wink with a golden grin,
As dusk arrives, the giggles spin.
Footprints fading, but fun remains,
In memories bright, like wild refrains.

The Color of Laughter

A palette bright with giggles and cheer,
Orange giggles and laughter so near.
Green chuckles splash, red blushes bloom,
Colors dance 'round, dispelling the gloom.

Blue waves crash with a cheeky clap,
Joking with the shore, in a playful flap.
Yellow sunbeams tickle the air,
While purple whispers tease without care.

Cotton candy clouds drift with glee,
As laughter floats like a buoy at sea.
Each hue a chuckle, each shade a jest,
Crafting smiles in a color-fueled fest.

Painting joy with wild strokes and swirls,
Laughter is the ink that twirls and whirls.
In a rainbow of giggles, let's find our way,
Coloring life with the jokes we play.

Cascade of Ocean Colors

Waves tumble down in a giggling spree,
Brilliant blues, a joke from the sea.
Fishes wink with bubbles so round,
A chorus of chuckles from deep underground.

Coral dances in a vibrant jig,
A clownfish performs, doing a big twig.
Seaweed sways with a quirky flair,
Tugging on toes, like it's beyond compare.

Shells tap-dance on the sandy floor,
While dolphins flip and beg for more.
Jellyfish float, with a silly grace,
Each tendril waving, a jelly-filled lace.

The ocean's laughter, a symphony bright,
A cascade of colors that feel just right.
Every wave whispers a playful jest,
In this splashy world, we're truly blessed.

Reverie in a Hibiscus Garden

In a garden lush, where blooms seem to tease,
Hibiscus giggles ride on a breeze.
Petals flutter in a comical way,
As bees buzz funny tunes through the day.

A sunflower stretches, tall and spry,
Telling jokes to the clouds up high.
Butterflies flutter with colorful grace,
Dancing and laughing in a joyful race.

A cheeky breeze gives the leaves a shake,
Whispering secrets that make flowers quake.
Laughter fills air like sweet perfume,
In this garden of dreams, we joyfully bloom.

As night descends with a mischievous wink,
Stars join in, covering all with a blink.
In the softness of petals, let's lose our fears,
A garden of laughter, we'll plant our cheers.

Dreams Weave Through Palms

The coconut fell with a soft thud,
A monkey just shrugged with a chuckle.
"I thought it was a round fruit, not a dud!"
But he tossed it aside, quick as a buckle.

The sand was hot, the surf was grand,
A crab tried to dance, oh what a sight!
He clutched his claws like he planned a band,
But slipped and flipped, oh what a fright!

The sun wore shades, the sky played games,
While umbrellas flipped like angry fish.
Each shadow at noon had silly names,
As kites tangled with a piñata wish.

We laughed at the breeze that blew our hats,
It played hide-and-seek with every stride.
We might be sweet, just like juicy sprats,
But we're all clowns on this wild ride!

Colorful Chimeras of the Coast

A parrot named Bob wore a scarf so bright,
He tried to sing, but sounded like crabs.
Each note was a struggle, a fluttering fright,
While seagulls laughed and made passing jabs.

The waves were giggling, they tickled the sand,
Jellyfish jigged like they owned the scene.
In the swirl of surf, they took a grand stand,
While tourists snapped pics, hoping for sheen.

A sandcastle stood, with a moat quite grand,
But fell to a wave like a nerd at a prom.
Little shells danced, holding hands on the strand,
And waved goodbye, alarmed by the calm.

We feasted on coconuts, hearts full of cheer,
As the tide reset, and the sun wore a grin.
Each moment was vivid, bright, full of cheer,
In this riot of color where nonsense begins.

Enigma of the Mangrove Forest

In the mangrove maze where the lizards lie,
A frog attempted to tell a tall tale.
But each croak echoed underneath the blue sky,
And he paused mid-yawn, lost in his trail.

The roots intertwined like a grappling hook,
Fish peeked out, playing hide-and-seek games.
"What's next?" asked a crab, with a curious look,
"Does this lead to treasures or just more names?"

A heron in shades strutted with pizzazz,
Claiming real estate on a half-sunk log.
But before long, he had to take a pizzazz,
As a gopher tortoise came by like a fog.

Trees whispered secrets, and the waters twirled,
We stumbled through laughter, in this leafy zoo.
Where the sun crowned each mischief, our hearts unfurled,
Creativity ruled and our minds flew on cue.

Silhouettes Against the Sunset

At dusk the sky danced, a mango melange,
Children giggled, dragons flew wide.
Their laughter painted the sunset's strange,
As the day wore off its childish pride.

A turtle raced slow, not quite in the game,
While the sunset sighed, saying, "Take it slow!"
The flamingos flapped, preening with fame,
As crickets tuned up for the evening show.

Starfish sat still, like old sleepy guards,
While fish shared secrets with waves of delight.
They all seemed to laugh, and count all the cards,
In this silhouetted, shimmering night.

We sang to the sea, our voices so brave,
As dreams tied us close, like a warm cozy string.
The ocean whispered, "No one's too grave,"
In the gloaming's glow, let your heart take wing!

The Call of the Island Songbirds

In the morning, birds chant loud,
Serenading a sloth so proud.
Coconuts fall with a plop,
As monkeys dance and hop, hop, hop.

The parrot cackles with glee,
As crabs join in the spree.
A lizard gives a cheeky wink,
While sipping on a drink so pink.

Karaoke night on the beach,
With island folk who love to screech.
The sea turtle steals the show,
With moves that make the waves go 'whoa!'

Under stars, laughter flows,
As everybody knows.
In this place of singing cheer,
You'd need an extra ear!

Silken Roads through Jade Leaves

Wandering paths of emerald green,
Where every leaf is fit for a queen.
Frogs croak silly serenades,
While grasshoppers flaunt their charades.

A breeze whispers, tickles the trees,
Stirring giggles in the warm, soft breeze.
Chasing shadows, a lizard darts,
While ants hold a parade of parts.

In this kingdom of vibrant bliss,
Even the flowers share a kiss.
Bumblebees buzz in crazy loops,
Dancing with the hanging fruit scoops.

On trails of silk and shining light,
Everything seems just so right.
With laughter echoing, who could blame?
Happiness here plays a game!

A Journey to the Heart of Paradise

Through wind and waves, we sail away,
Chasing rainbows at the break of day.
Finding treasures, big or small,
Cooking up mischief; we'll have a ball!

Sandy toes and pineapple hats,
Somersaulting like the acrobats.
Seahorses giggle, riding the tide,
As fish join the fun, swimming side by side.

The sun is a jester, playing a trick,
Making shadows that dance and kick.
We feast on fritters, sweet and bright,
Till the moon shines down with a wink of light.

Every moment is wild and free,
Like a surfer's wave on a cotton candy spree.
With laughter and joy, we sing out loud,
In the heart of this merry crowd!

Lullabies of the Coconut Trees

Underneath the tall trees sway,
Coconuts chat and play all day.
A squirrel tells tales, held in awe,
While crickets chirp like the great law.

Nighttime falls; the fireflies blink,
Lighting up secrets we'll never think.
With sleepy waves that rock the shore,
A serenade from the ocean floor.

Palms stretch their arms, yawning wide,
As frogs croon lullabies with pride.
Sleepyheads snuggle in sandy beds,
With coconut dreams in their heads!

The stars giggle above so bright,
As everyone drifts into the night.
In the hush, a soft tale spins,
In this land where the fun begins!

The Flavor of Sunset Sangria

In a glass, a splash of cheer,
Red like my neighbor's pet deer.
Fruits float like clouds up high,
I sip, and pretend to fly.

This drink tastes like a festival,
Bursting flavors, so festively typical.
I slurp while practicing my dance,
The geraniums blush at my chance.

Lemon twists and berries tease,
Why do they giggle? Just sip with ease.
Maybe it's the sun in my cup,
Or the dancing ants who never give up!

I'll toast to nights that never end,
When a froggy friend squeaks 'let's blend!'
With each sip, I'm off the ground,
In this silly place where stars abound.

Raindrops on Swaying Palms

Raindrops plink on leafy screens,
Dance party for slugs and beans.
Each drop's a plucky little face,
Splashing joy in this warm embrace.

Palms sway like epic dance pros,
Shaking off their rainy woes.
The sun peeks, a curious fellow,
As puddles mirror my wild yellow.

Wind whispers secrets, light as air,
It tickles my toes, gives me a scare.
Those raindrops laugh with every tap,
Making me wonder, "Should I nap?"

So here I twirl, a joyous chap,
Finding harmony in puddled maps.
Each ripple spins a tale anew,
Of raindrops that dream with skies so blue.

Echoes of the Night Market

Cobblestones hum, a market alive,
Where every vendor makes taste buds thrive.
Spices entwined with shouts and cheer,
A circus for all who wander near.

Bright lanterns dance like fireflies,
And sweet snacks wink with eager sighs.
I barter smiles for sticky treats,
In this bazaar of questionable feats.

A mango falls, it rolls my way,
Does it want me to join the display?
I tackle it, laughter takes flight,
As drumbeats echo through the night.

With each taste, a quirky delight,
I clap my hands, feeling just right.
The market whispers, "Here's some fun!"
I grin, munching 'til the day is done.

Sipping Dreams from Pineapple Cups

A pineapple crowned, my drink divine,
It whispers, "Take a sip, feel fine!"
With each slurp, I giggle and sway,
Is it the drink or the sun's ballet?

Coconut friends wear silly hats,
While papayas gossip with playful chats.
Sipping dreams, oh what a thrill,
This fruity giggle gives me a chill.

In this cup, the sea does sing,
As mermaids join in the tropical swing.
I sprinkle in joy, a dash of spice,
And toast to mischief, oh so nice!

With every drop, I'm lost in bliss,
Floating on waves of pineapple kiss.
What day is it? Oh, who even cares?
I'm dancing with fruit in leafy lairs!

Jaunt through the Jasmine Fields

In a field of jasmine, I slipped on a bee,
Tried to sneak by quietly, oh dear, oh me!
The flowers all giggled, a raucous affair,
As I fell on my backside, head full of air.

Butterflies danced, what a sight to behold,
I attempted to impress, but my antics grew old.
With petals in my hair like a floral crown,
I looked quite the sight, a spectacle in town.

The sun cast its glow, a mischievous spark,
As I stumbled and tumbled, oh what a lark!
The scent in the air, both sweet and absurd,
I laughed with the flowers, their whispers unheard.

The Breeze's Gentle Caress

A breeze came a-chuckling, tickling my nose,
Waltzing with my hat, oh where did it go?
It danced on a cloud, with a wink and a tease,
While I chased after it, I tripped on a freeze!

The sun's laughing too, it's a merry affair,
As I tangle with branches, imagining air.
I looked to the skies, while birds cackled in glee,
'Running amok!' they sang, 'Just let yourself be!'

The breeze whispered secrets, a playful delight,
In this windy chaos, I twirled with delight.
While the world spun around in a giggling spree,
I basked in the silliness, just my hat and me.

Echoes of Tropical Rain

Raindrops like marbles came crashing with glee,
I slipped on the pavement, a slip-n-slide spree!
Puddles were dancing, reflecting the gray,
As I let out a squeal, in the splashes I play.

The thunder rolled softly, a beat to the cheer,
Like nature was laughing at my wild fear.
With each joyful splash, I let out a grin,
Surrounded by laughter, my rain dance begin.

Oh, how the plants giggled, in laughter they swayed,
As I made my grand entrance, a shower parade.
With shoes full of water and joy in my heart,
I twirled in the rain, a whimsical art.

Luminous Paths beneath the Palms

Underneath the palms where the shadows do twirl,
I tried to impress, but my feet took a whirl.
With the coconuts chuckling, I made quite the scene,
As I stumbled and fumbled, a slapstick routine.

The lights in the sky began winking and bright,
While I fancied a dance, oh what a delight!
But my legs had their own plans, they just wouldn't comply,
As I toppled once more, and giggles passed by.

The moon watched in wonder, a spotlight on me,
As I jived with the stars, a clumsy jubilee.
With laughter surrounding, I leapt and I spun,
In this luminous chaos, we all had such fun.

Sunsets Stitched with Wishes

Banana peels on sidewalks gleam,
Laughter echoes, a joyful theme.
Coconuts dance on ocean tides,
While crabs do the cha-cha in playful strides.

Flip-flops fling with every leap,
As seagulls gossip, secrets to keep.
Sunsets wear a vibrant hue,
While margaritas spill, a colorful brew.

Chasing shadows beneath palm trees,
We twirl like whirlwinds in the breeze.
A frisbee sails, a dog in pursuit,
Life's a parade in flip-flop suit.

Moonlight winks, the stars align,
As dreams take flight on a swing divine.
With giggles shared and breezy sighs,
Our hearts are stitched in laughter's ties.

Wandering Through a Garden of Gold

Marigolds giggle, sunflowers sway,
We skip through petals, at play all day.
With bees in bowties, buzzing around,
And butterflies prancing, lost and found.

The garden gnomes guard silly hats,
While bunnies hop in acrobatic spats.
Tomatoes wear shades, looking so fine,
As carrots do limbo beneath the vine.

A garden hose plays a sneaky trick,
Spraying laughter as we dance quick.
In this patch of joy, we plant our dreams,
With laughter spilling in glittering streams.

As twilight drapes in hues of blue,
We gather 'round for tea brewed anew.
With cookies shaped like silly clowns,
The fun in this garden never drowns.

Perpetual Summer's Embrace

Sunhats tipped and shades askew,
We strut like peacocks, a colorful crew.
With flip-flops tapping to a lively beat,
We twist and twirl on warm, sandy sheets.

Ice cream drips like laughter flows,
While sunburnt noses reap what they sow.
A piña colada steals a sly kiss,
As we juggle our dreams in a sun-kissed bliss.

Surfers carve waves with ocean flair,
While beach balls bounce through salty air.
A seagull swoops, steals a fry,
As we chuckle and shout, oh my, oh my!

Evenings draped in golden light,
We roast marshmallows, laughter takes flight.
With stories spun of ridiculous schemes,
Life here is better than our wildest dreams.

Mysteries in the Twilight Glow

Lanterns flicker with mischief's charm,
As shadows whisper, oh so warm.
With night-blooming flowers that giggle and tease,
And fireflies twirling like twinkling keys.

We dance on the sand with feet so bare,
As crickets play tunes in the balmy air.
A coconut falls with a thud and a laugh,
While we map the stars on a driftwood path.

Ghost crabs scuttle with wobbly grace,
As moonbeams paint smiles on each face.
The tides carry secrets from far and wide,
With treasures of laughter we try to abide.

At midnight's peak, a comet zooms,
Sending wishes that burst like bloons.
With hearts alight and gleeful eyes,
We chase the mysteries that light up the skies.

Lush Lullabies of the Landscape

In a hammock strung from two tall trees,
I snooze my worries, swing with ease.
Mangoes giggle as they fall,
And pineapples are having a ball.

Parrots squawk, they jest and tease,
While I sip juice, feeling the breeze.
A coconut rolls, oh, what a sight!
It seems to dance in pure delight.

The sun throws a party, oh so bright,
Beach towels wearing shades with all their might.
A crab in sunglasses struts along,
Singing to waves, quite the silly song.

A lizard in flip flops tries to race,
But ends up tangled in a leaf chase.
With laughter echoing far and wide,
This landscape's a stage, and we're the pride.

Sweet Epiphanies in Paradise

A koala on a vine takes a snack,
Why does it munch with such a knack?
The sun spills juice on my freshly baked bread,
It's the best jam I never had spread.

Turtles in shades, oh what a sight,
Waddling slow like they own the night.
A runaway flip-flop plays hide-and-seek,
While flamingos practice their dance technique.

Got a pineapple on my head, it's true,
I'm the crown prince, who knew?
Bananas are laughing, giving me cheek,
Nature's fun joke has me feeling unique.

Melons roll by in a sunny parade,
While I sip coconuts, slightly delayed.
With each silly twist of fate, I find,
Sweet revelations wrap around my mind.

Fireflies and Fountains of Light

Fireflies flicker, a glowing charade,
As frogs join in with their serenade.
The night soggy with shimmering sparks,
While I chase my dreams through the parks.

A fountain leaps up, with giggles galore,
Splashing all over—who could ask for more?
A fish wears a hat, what a peculiar sight,
As petals pirouette in the soft moonlight.

With laughter that bounces off every tree,
I see a snail in a race, oh me!
The fireflies dance like they know a joke,
Nature's own comedy, a warm, fuzzy cloak.

A lizard adjusted his little bow tie,
While a parrot jokes—oh me, oh my!
This bubbly night is a whimsical tease,
With fireflies and fountains, laughter's a breeze.

Rhythms of a Casuarina Breeze

Casuarinas sway to a jazzy tune,
As I twirl about like a crazy cartoon.
A squirrel with shades hops close to my bag,
While seagulls gossip with a wag.

Coconuts drop like beats from the sky,
I catch them laughing at my failed try.
Jellyfish are bobbing in a synchronized line,
Waving to me, saying, "When will you dine?"

The breeze blows gentle, a playful caress,
Whispers of coconut cream, nothing less.
As I break into fits of silly rhyme,
I feel like a jester in the pocket of time.

With rhythm and giggles, we dance and we play,
The breezy melodies take worries away.
In this quirkiest land of happy surprise,
Life's just a fun show, oh, just look at the skies!

Celestial Symphony Above the Canopy

The monkeys in tango up in the trees,
Swinging and howling, they dance with the breeze.
Parrots in hats, they squawk with delight,
Wearing their colors so bold and so bright.

Beneath the banana, a picnic spread wide,
With sandwiches flying off, oh, what a ride!
A beetle in shades is sipping cold tea,
While ants in tuxedos hold a grand spree.

The coconut dances, a pirouette twist,
While crabs start a conga—it could not be missed!
A party of creatures, all laughing in sync,
Who knew jungle life could be so on the brink?

As moonbeams come down, they join in the fun,
A wild, wacky shindig under the sun.
Up in the canopy, laughter does soar,
In this merry realm, who could ask for more?

Echoes of a Sunlit Retreat

Palm trees are swaying with giggles afloat,
As lizards parade in their fanciest coat.
A crab taps his shoes on the hot sandy floor,
While turtles with sunglasses start up a score.

The sea brings a siren, with songs that they croon,
She juggles some shells while the fish hum a tune.
A jellyfish joins in with glimmers of class,
As it twirls through the water, with all of its sass.

A picnic's afoot, with cakes piled on high,
But a seagull swoops down with a glee in its eye.
It snatches a donut, what cheek, what dare!
Leaving puzzled beachgoers just shaking in air.

Under the sun where the laughter can soar,
Life's never so serious, oh, we beg for more!
In this goofy retreat by the sea so divine,
We dance with the waves, as we sip on sweet wine.

Garland of Memories by the Shore

Seashells are laughing, each one has a tale,
As crabs in formation set up a grand scale.
With winks and with nudges, they throw quite a bash,
A parade of the quirkiest, oh, what a smash!

The wind whispers secrets to kites in the sky,
While children are chasing a wayward fry.
With flip-flops and giggles, they dash through the foam,
Sandcastles tumble in laughter, they roam.

A buoy in a tutu spins round on the sea,
In this world of oddities, we're all young and free.
Mothers just smile as they watch all the fun,
While dads take their naps under bright, gleaming sun.

At night, when the stars sprinkle tales in the dark,
The waves whisper stories, and we feel the spark.
With hearts full of memories, we drift into dreams,
In this place by the shore, nothing's as it seems.

The Allure of Wandering Tides

A clam in a fedora debates with a tide,
While starfish are laughing, you know they can't hide.
They plan a big heist on a pile of lost shoes,
With shells as their briefing and sand as their clues.

The waves throw their foam like a playful dog,
While dolphins dive down in a splashy fog.
Each splash brings a giggle, a splutter, a cheer,
As mermaids in flippers draw everyone near.

With coconuts rolling like balls in the sand,
And parrots debating who leads the band.
The charm of the coast, all so silly yet sweet,
Keeps everyone smiling and bouncing to beat.

So come take a stroll where the tides come and go,
Let laughter prevail and your worries be slow.
With smiles at the shores and waves all around,
In this blend of humor, true joy can be found.

Mango Hues and Ocean Breezes

Mangoes fall like laughter, sweet,
Sun-kissed cheeks in summer heat.
Cocktails dance on sandy shores,
While seagulls steal your lunch galore.

Flip-flops flop and giggles soar,
Sunburned noses want some more.
Konks blow tunes of blissful cheer,
As crabs plot pranks, it's clear.

Waves invite with frothy smiles,
While sandcastles rest for miles.
Sandy toes with funny tales,
Dance with joy, like silly snails.

So grab your shades and catch a breeze,
Live along with silly tease.
Mangoes, waves, and laughter's song,
In this place, we all belong.

The Laughter of Palms

Palm trees waltz and sway with ease,
Tickling clouds and teasing bees.
Their leaves join in a playful jest,
As winds hum tunes, they never rest.

Fronds wave hello, a cheeky greet,
While coconuts roll at your feet.
Dance of shadows on the ground,
In this humor, joy is found.

Squirrels chatter, plotting schemes,
Under sunlit laughter beams.
Palms sway gently, wink and grin,
A comedy of nature's kin.

Join the fun, don't miss the show,
Let your laughter freely flow.
In this grove of mimicry,
Life's a jest, oh can't you see?

Swaying Hearts in Paradise

Hearts a-sway with shimmy flair,
Sun-kissed dreams float in warm air.
Cockatoos boast of silly plans,
While sunburned tourists take their tans.

Limbo contests spark the night,
Who can bend without a fright?
As laughter fills the starry skies,
The island hums with joyful cries.

Hammocks swing with gentle sway,
Hosting naps that steal the day.
When iguanas wear shades around,
You know this place is joy profound.

With carefree tunes that catch your ear,
Dance, my friend, and hold your beer!
In every corner, bliss is found,
As swaying hearts spin round and round.

Whispering Waves at Dusk

Waves whisper secrets, soft and sweet,
Tickling toes like a playful greet.
With sunset hues that make you grin,
Each splash a giggle, let's begin.

Shells on the sand are little jokes,
While crabs engage in silly pokes.
The horizon blushes, quite a sight,
As the moon peeks in, all dressed in light.

Whimsical boats with funny names,
Rocking gently in watery games.
The smell of treats that tickles your nose,
A feast of laughter, love, and prose.

So let the waves sing you to sleep,
As starlit dreams begin to creep.
In this realm where joy is found,
Every whisper makes the heart bounce around.

A Cauldron of Sweet Sours

In a pot of confusion, bananas dance,
While coconuts giggle, plotting romance.
Papayas wear hats made of zest and cheer,
Limes throw confetti, "What a party here!"

Mangoes slide down like slick little spies,
Passion fruits gossip, sharing their lies.
Guavas in sandals, they waddle and sway,
"Who ate the sunshine?"—a fruit buffet play!

Chili peppers argue, "We're hot, can't you see?"
While cilantro looks lost, as lost as can be.
A fruit salad ruckus, with laughs on the side,
In this crazy cauldron, all sweetness can't hide.

Banana peels slip on their merry old fate,
As everyone swirls in a fruity debate.
From tangy to sweet, they embrace mischief well,
In this pot of whimsy, all flavors compel.

Canvas of the Casuarina Coast.

Under the trees with a light breezy sigh,
Seagulls are sneezing, oh my, oh my!
Canvas stretched wide with colors so bright,
Sandy toes flutter, what a silly sight!

Crabs march in line, all dressed up for tea,
"Is it crabby or crab-cake?" they question with glee.
The ocean laughs back, waves rolling in fun,
Painting the beach as they soak up the sun.

Coconuts chuckle, they drop with a plop,
While flip-flops scatter, "It's time for a hop!"
Dancing on sand, it's a quirky parade,
With a splash and a giggle, the artwork is made!

Shells whisper secrets, "What's fresh on the beach?"
"Did you hear the rumors?" they always impeach.
A canvas of laughter, color, and cheer,
On this coast of absurdity, no frown interferes.

Island Whispers

Shells gossip softly, secrets they share,
A crab in a tuxedo, what a strange wear!
The winds play games with the palm's silly hats,
While iguanas dance, gossiping like chitchats.

"Who's stealing the fruit?" cries the pineapple stout,
As mangoes unite, they mutter and pout.
Coconuts wobble, fearing the rain,
"What if we float off? Oh, is that a pain?"

The sun sticks its tongue out, pouring down cheer,
While the sea turtles giggle, "We're out of here!"
Islanders chuckle, on pedicabs they ride,
Tropical whispers are full of wild pride.

Every corner a joke, every shadow a smile,
Within this lush paradise, silly all the while.
From banana boats rocking to jellyfish games,
Each whisper tells tales of mischief and names.

Sun-Kissed Shores

Upon the warm sands, where shadows do prance,
Sunglasses giggle as they have a chance.
With flippers and fins, fish take a big leap,
"Out of the water!" they shout, "No time for sleep!"

Surfers in tutus ride waves with delight,
While flip-flops are lost in the splashy fight.
Seagulls wear shades, they strut and they screech,
"Let's dive for treasure or hunt for a peach!"

The horizon shimmers, as kites dance and twirl,
While beach balls bounce in a carefree swirl.
Sunscreen is flying, on toes, arms, and nose,
As laughter erupts, this blissful chaos grows.

In the warmth of the sun, all worries evade,
With a splash and a dash, life's foolish charade.
Sun-kissed and goofy, we bask in the glow,
"Who needs a reason?" they gleefully crow.

Whispers of the Sunlit Shore

Seagulls squawking, what a surprise,
A crab in a hat, oh me, oh my!
Sandcastles crumble, the tide gives chase,
While I'm busy forming a sunburned face.

Flip-flops flapping, I shuffle along,
Finding a conch that sings me a song.
Seashells giggle, they're having a ball,
But I trip on my towel and tumble—whoops! Fall!

Lemonade spills, sticky on my nose,
A fish wearing shades just glared at my toes.
Palm trees chuckle, swaying with glee,
While I'm lost in a dance with a bumblebee!

The sunset winks, paints the sky bright,
Alligators in shades slide quietly by.
As laughter lingers in the air above,
Nature whispers sweetly, sharing its love.

Mango Moonlight Serenade

Under the stars with a mango in hand,
I dance with a lizard, it's all rather grand.
Fireflies twinkle like disco balls,
While the moon plays music, and all nature sprawls.

Mangoes are rolling, they think it's a race,
I chase after one, it takes me a pace.
The frogs are all croaking, but wait—what's that?
A parrot in flip-flops, oh fancy that!

With every bite, I declare, "What a treat!"
Except when the juice flows all down my feet.
The night grows richer with laughter and cheer,
As the stars throw a party; they're all gathered here!

Time for a dance, the moon's glowing bright,
I question my steps in this whimsical night.
With laughter and mangos, this night's a delight,
What's funnier than joy? Nothing feels right!

Lush Oasis Reverie

In a pool made of coconuts, sipping with flair,
The fishes are gossiping without a care.
Palm leaves discreetly are planning a show,
While I plop in nose-first—oh where did I go?

A turtle in shades gives a thumbs-up to me,
Not sure if he's laughing or lost in the sea.
Watermelons float like they own the place,
While I struggle to keep my cool and my grace.

The breeze brings whispers of fruit and of sun,
I'm caught in a splash fight—thing's just begun!
The iguanas watch, they are all dressed in style,
I'm flinging my arms and they cringe for a while.

As the sunset declares, "Hey, life isn't gray!"
I laugh with the critters, bright colors at play.
In this lush oasis, my worries all flee,
With joy all around, who needs a degree?

Coconut Clouds and Waves

Riding a wave of coconut cream,
I bubble and giggle, it feels like a dream.
Plenty of giggles and mischief ahead,
That seagull just stole my churro, I said!

Waves crash like laughter on soft sandy shores,
I'm gathering shells while life playfully roars.
A crab steals a flip-flop, as quick as a wink,
While I'm trying to figure out how to think!

Pineapples dance in the warm ocean spray,
Jellyfish float by, with flair, not a sway.
A hammock's a trap for the best kind of fun,
Until I drift off and forget the sun!

But laughter still lingers, carried by breeze,
As coconuts chuckle, and sway with such ease.
In this world full of joy, with laughter and glee,
Each wave tells a tale, come join the spree!

Chasing the Breeze of Serenity

In the hammock I sway, quite a sight,
Chasing dragonflies on a sunny flight.
The mangoes drop down, and oh what a mess,
I catch them with glee, I must confess!

The pineapple hat fits like a crown,
I strut on the beach, not a care in town.
The seagulls caw loud, they think they're the best,
While I dance with my shadow, a silly request!

Azure Skies and Golden Shores

With toes in the sand, I waddle and flop,
Collecting bright seashells, like a clumsy shop.
The sun-belting laughter, it tickles my nose,
I do the conga while the crab just doze!

A smoothie in hand, it spills on my lap,
I giggle at seagulls who snatch up my cap.
The waves tease my ankles and splash like a jest,
As I try to look cool, but fail with zest!

The Rhythm of the Island Breeze

Whirling like a dervish, I twirl with delight,
The breeze gives a tug, oh what a flight!
A coconut falls with a bumbling thud,
And I tumble right after, face first in the mud!

The palm trees just shake, they're having a laugh,
As I chase my wide-brimmed hat, oh what a gaffe!
The ukulele strums, and I march in place,
Trying to salsa while stuck in this space!

Caress of the Warm Sea

The ocean waves giggle, they pull on my leg,
In a splash of cool water, I dance like a peg.
Flip-flops go flying, they're lost in the tide,
While I chase after fish, feeling bright and wide!

A seahorse winks, with a mischievous smile,
We twirl and we whirl, in an underwater trial.
My snorkel is crooked, I can't see a thing,
But I laugh with the fishes, oh what joy they bring!

A Taste of Golden Sunsets

The sun dips low, a mango grin,
Bouncing on waves, let the fun begin.
Rum drinks in hand, a conga line,
Salsa and laughter, oh, ain't life fine!

A parrot squawks a silly tune,
Dancing with dolphins beneath the moon.
Laughter erupts, a beach party spree,
Who needs a plan? Just let it be!

Sandy toes and a coconut hat,
Chasing crabs, oh, how 'bout that?
Jellyfish waltz, a curious sight,
Sunsets taste sweeter when you're feeling light!

Pouring bright colors into the sky,
Flip-flops flying, oh my, oh my!
With every sip and silly cheer,
Golden hour, bring on the beer!

The Caress of Mist in the Morning

Waking up to a misty brew,
Coffee spills like gossip, it's true!
Parrots stealing sugar, so bold,
Laughter and sunshine, a story unfold.

The breeze whispers jokes, can you hear?
Tickling the palm trees, oh dear!
Chasing the fog like a playful cat,
Pretending I'm swimming in a giant hat!

Flipping pancakes, a pancake parade,
Sticky syrup, don't let it fade!
A jellyfish flops, a slapstick act,
In the morning mist, life's never abstract.

The sun peeks in, another round,
Time to explore the laughs abound!
With giggles and dreams in the air,
Misty mornings, oh what a flair!

Daydreams by the Beach

Shells and sandcastles, a kingdom of fun,
Seagulls playing tag, under the sun.
Daydreams flutter like kites in the sky,
With coconut drinks, oh my oh my!

A crab walks sideways, a clumsy jest,
Waving at surfers, who's doing their best.
Fish chasing waves, they leap and flop,
In this sandy sitcom, we never stop!

With sunscreen as armor, let's dive and splash,
Laughter and friendship, in a joyful rush.
Rainbows of laughter, oh, what a treat,
Life's better served with a side of sweet!

As the sun dips low, we plot our next prank,
A treasure hunt's coming, let's fill up the tank!
Giggles echo, as night starts to creep,
Daydreams by the beach, it's fun, not cheap!

Vibrant Echoes of the Tropics

Bright colors bounce like a playful song,
Dancing on breezes, all day long.
Palms sway and giggle, in perfect sync,
Brewed coffee hiccups, mix with a wink!

Bamboo flutes whistle a hilarious tune,
While monkeys parade 'neath the big round moon.
With every swing and parties galore,
It's a circus show, who could ask for more?

Watermelon smiles and beach ball fights,
Sun-kissed moments on sparkling nights.
In vibrant echoes, wild stories emerge,
As the wild waves crash, oh let's splurge!

Catch that wave, ride it high,
Laughter's the secret to never say goodbye.
In this paradise, let your spirit roam,
With every giggle, we find our home!

www.ingramcontent.com/pod-product-compliance
Lightning Source LLC
Chambersburg PA
CBHW072128070526
44585CB00016B/1571